BOOK OF ADVANCED QUINTETS
With discussion and techniques

EDITED and ARRANGED by
Walter H. Barnes

Arranged for:
1st (B♭) Trumpet
➤ 2nd (B♭) Trumpet
Horn in F
Trombone
Tuba
Conductor

THE CANADIAN BRASS EDUCATIONAL SERIES

Copyright © 1986 Canadian Brass Publications, Toronto
International Copyright Secured. ALL RIGHTS RESERVED.

THE CANADIAN BRASS

Book of advanced quintets
With discussion and techniques

EDITED and ARRANGED by
Walter H. Barnes

Contents

E   Easy   M   Medium   D   Difficult

A 'note' to you

We are very pleased to offer you this Advanced Book of Quintets. It is the third in our Educational Series, preceded by the Beginning and the Easy Quintet books, and is especially compiled for the serious brass student. We believe that the fourteen pieces that we have chosen are an excellent representation from the world of keyboard, vocal, and instrumental writing spanning four centuries. Many of the works parallel our own repertoire: the Stanley Trumpet Voluntary is very similar to some of our Purcell recordings; the Fantasia and Fugue is scored exactly like our Toccata and Fugue in D minor; Hallelujah, Amen is reminiscent of our Hallelujah Chorus; Pinafore is typical of many of the orchestral scores that we have arranged for quintet. The selections in this collection are playable on B flat trumpets and tuba, double horn and tenor trombone. And all of these pieces are within the capabilities of a well-balanced quintet or ensemble of High School students. (Our own repertoire is published under the Canadian Brass Brassworks Series and will be suitable for you when you have conquered this book.)

We ask that you consider all elements contained in this list:

tone
tuning
timing
technique
balance
blend
musicality

Every time that you play any note, you must produce the very best tone possible. The tone must characterize the style of the piece, and compliment your group. It is *your musical fingerprint*. It is probably the most important single quality in the presentation of a solo. But when playing quintet music, it must be coupled with tuning. Tuning gains in importance through duet, trio, and quartet. It probably reaches its summit of greatest difficulty in quintet, and then receives less care and attention unfortunately as the numbers increase from chamber group to concert band. We have suggested throughout that you constantly tune to the tuba, the foundation, as well as those beside you.

Balance and blend within your ensemble must be a variable depending on the selection and the scoring. And you must constantly be aware of its value. A solo should be dominant, but it must be well supported by the other four instruments. In our rehearsals, we are always aware of what the other person is playing, and how our musical partnerships are developed. In our notes to you, we have placed great importance on supporting roles (not subordinate roles). Please re-read these comments as you progress through each piece, and consider your balance, colour, and blend. As well, the timing of notes and rests (musical silences) is of utmost importance in order to achieve a unity of sound and pulse.

And, finally, with your increasing competence through consistent practice, the 'soul' of the skill becomes the art-form. The notes are shaped into phrases, sentences, and paragraphs; the music is lifted from the page; the composer's initial communication turns into your own musical statement, now ready for performance.

There are a few details to note. Breath marks in parenthesis are to be used only if necessary, not for musical reasons. Cues are given for most rests, so that you are more aware of what your partners play. And, finally, we have recorded this book on cassette — available from your music dealer — so that we can perform your pieces for you, and put into music what we have tried to explain through words and symbols.

Have fun!

The Canadian Brass

Trumpet Voluntary

JOHN STANLEY

John Stanley was a famous English organist and composer. Although he was a contemporary of Handel, his writing related more to Purcell, many years his predecessor. He wrote many organ voluntaries, cantatas, concertos, and even two oratorios — surprising, in that he was blind from the age of two!

Stanley was very highly respected for his performances on the organ. It was not uncommon for fifty other organists, with Handel himself included, to gather in the Temple Church and listen to the final voluntary of the service played by Stanley.

A quaint definition of 'Voluntary' as found in ELEMENTS OF MUSIC, published in 1772 during Stanley's lifetime, follows:

"A grand Piece of Musick, performed on the Organ, which is (or ought to be) solemn, grand, and noble withal; free from all antick or lascivious Airs, which only corrupt the mind with impure Thoughts. It should call in our Spirits, delight our Ears, and recreate our Minds, giving us a Taste of Heaven, here on Earth."

C.B.

This is a difficult piece for the second trumpet. At times, you are a soloist; at other times, you are in a supporting role. Watch that your dotted rhythms are exactly in a three-to-one ratio, and that you follow the first trumpet in style and timing. Bar 28 is a good example. Bars 31–36 gives you a chance for excellent ensemble playing with the french horn and the trombone. Relate your pitch and equality of rests (musical silences) with them. Complete the piece with a flourish at bars 64–66.

1. Trumpet Voluntary

Stanley
(1713-1786)

Trumpet Voluntary *continued*

Three Elizabethan Madrigals

The English Madrigal of the 16th Century owed its origin to that of the Italian school. However, the English madrigal became "naturalized" due to the peculiarities of the language and the touch of merriment. Thomas Morley (1557–1602) was unusually famous as a writer of joyous madrigals proclaiming the singer's love for another. Both 'My Bonny Lass' and 'Now Is the Month of Maying' are still constantly performed by small choirs, and are two of the finest examples of the "merry madrigal". John Dowland (1562–1626) wrote the madrigal 'Come Again; Sweet Love Doth Now Invite' extolling the greater aspects of courtship. "To see, to hear, to touch, to be in sweetest sympathy . . ." All five voices in the three madrigals are equal and sing their own melody; therefore, balance and blend are most important in the performance of this work.

C.B.

'My Bonny Lass' offers you an excellent opportunity for contrast: the first four bars are light, bright, and detached; the four bars starting at the pick-up to bar 10 must show your singing and blending quality. Watch your entry at bar 44; play soloistically, with a slight detachment of the third note.

'Sweet Love Doth Now Invite' poses a real challenge for tuning and needs a consistent air column in the lower range. Remember: the lower the note, the more air you need for a rich tone quality. Now, that's all fine, provided you keep firm control on dynamics; do not override the french horn, who has the melody.

'Now Is the Month of Maying' brings you to two major problems:

— tuning the false relationship in bar 108 and 114;
— entering correctly in bar 116 and 132.

Clap your rhythm while the first trumpet, french horn and tuba play. (The trombone also has a rhythmic difficulty.) You must develop a strong physical feeling for the entry, and have a secure mental understanding of the timing. It's difficult!

2. Three Elizabethan Madrigals

Morley
(1557–1602)

I. My Bonny Lass

8

II. Sweet Love Doth Now Invite

Dowland
(1562-1626)

III. Now is the Month of Maying

Morley
(1557–1602)

Hosanna to The Son of David

ORLANDO GIBBONS

Gibbons was one of the most celebrated composers and gifted organists of the Elizabethan period of English music. He was chiefly known for his choral and keyboard writing. His early training was at King's College as a chorister, and later as a student, obtaining his B. Mus. in 1606. In his short lifetime, he served the royalty of England as organist of the Chapel Royal, and later of Westminster Abbey. He died shortly after conducting the music for the funeral of James I in 1625. His music for viols, for organ, and for voice is characterized by a free-flowing imaginative line rarely heard before his time.

'Hosanna' is possibly the finest example of polyphonic* writing which emerged from Elizabethan England. Every part is equally treated in this forerunner of the fugue form, so we speak to you in one voice, just as you must perform the Hosanna in one voice, in different ranges.

Gibbons wrote the music set to the words of the population of Jerusalem who welcomed Christ to the city. The phrases ring out one after another like a peal of bells. So take your first phrase, (second trumpet: make your first note a half note just for this exercise) and play all together, starting together. Every person must play with the same length, the same weight, the same inflection. Keep this trick in mind as you work on the entire piece, so that every phrase imitates the 'subject' phrase. There is a brief homophonic** passage for two choirs beginning at bar 25; use this section as contrast to the polyphonic writing.

You will notice that the time signature changes from time to time. Gibbons wrote the music without bar lines. In modern notation, bar lines are inserted, but must not be interpreted as a framework for accentuation. The natural accentuation follows the musical phrase and appears in each part at a different beat of the bar.

Canadian Brass

* polyphony   : where the melody is in all parts, often at the same time.
** homophony: Music written with one part featured as the melody and the other parts serving as the accompaniment.

3. Hosanna to the Son of David

Gibbons
(1583-1625)

Antiphonal
(Hodie; Christus Natus Est)

JAN SWEELINCK

Like Gibbons, Sweelinck was known throughout Europe as a great organist. He was born and lived in Amsterdam most of his life. As a player and a teacher of organ, he was renowned; he was a forerunner of the fugue form, using the pedals of the organ to present the subject, and building up counter-subjects to compliment the theme. His choral writing culminates the intricate contrapuntal school of the late Renaissance, and leads to the beginnings of the Baroque period.

There is much in common in the styles of Sweelinck and Gibbons as characterized in the two selections that we have chosen. Both use polyphony, in which the players must imitate the 'subject' melody as it is initially presented. Sweelinck employs several contrasting sections of homophony to set apart the polyphony. Here, the instruments must sound as a brass choir. The piece is divided into four parts; the trombone, joined later by the first trumpet, introduces the homophonic phrase in three-four time. This is followed by different polyphonic statements in four-four time, gathering in complexity and concluding in a fanfare, again akin to a peal of bells.

Canadian Brass

4. Antiphonal
(Hodie, Christus Natus Est.)

Sweelinck
(1562-1621)

Antiphonal *continued*

Handel

Hallelujah, Amen was written as a chorus for full choir, and is from the Oratorio 'Judas Maccabaeus'. It is almost entirely in polyphonic writing with each part standing equally and independently. Therefore, each instrument must duplicate the style of the opening phrase as stated by the trombone and tuba. We have graphed two portions for you so that you can see the fugal writing, and the construction of the two-choir section.

C.B.

The other selection that we have chosen from the pen of Handel is a well-known aria, 'Where'er You Walk'. Here, the two trumpets, at times joined by the trombone, are assigned the obligato — the decoration, the icing on the cake. The motion is usually upwards, in parallel motion, and in thirds. While the melody (french horn) is stationary, the trumpets trace the arpeggio of the chord. The inherent dangers are in the natural faults of the instruments: your E' lipping is flat, and your G' lipping above that is sharp. As well, all the notes in those harmonics played with valves are similarly affected. So, tuning becomes a primary concern. (Example: bar 26)

Play each flourish together, listening carefully. An electronic tuner will help you in your private practice. Strive for a smoothness and a flow not unlike a violin's performance. Treat the slurs more as phrase marks with the second note having less weight. Above all, never cover the solo with your decoration.

Hallelujah, Amen

(from "*Judas Maccabaeus*")

Handel

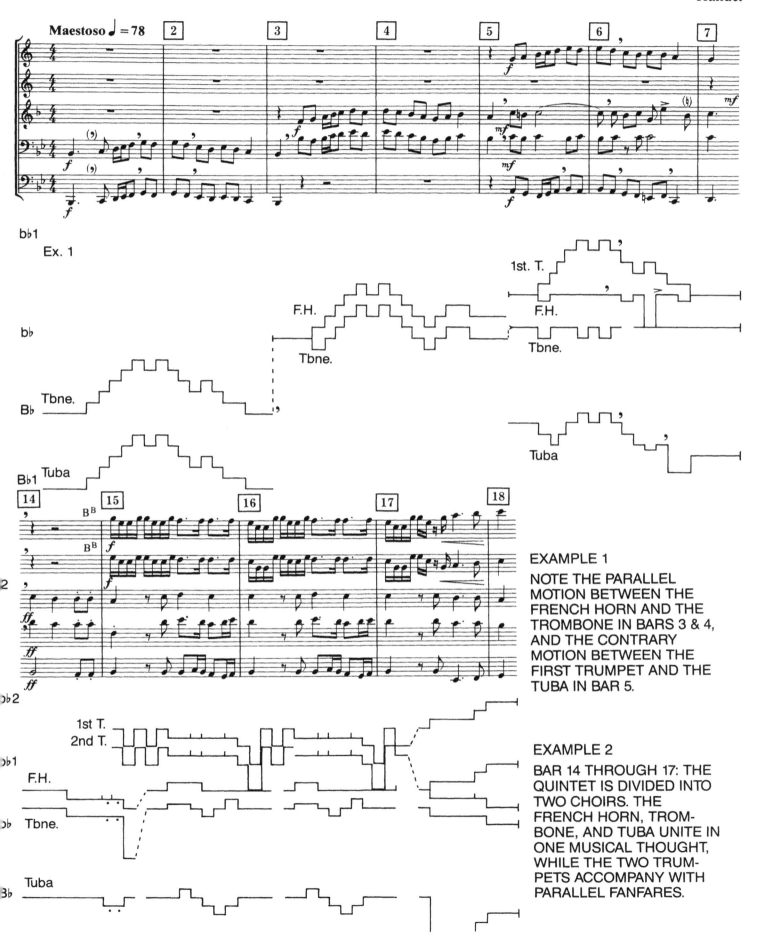

EXAMPLE 1

NOTE THE PARALLEL MOTION BETWEEN THE FRENCH HORN AND THE TROMBONE IN BARS 3 & 4, AND THE CONTRARY MOTION BETWEEN THE FIRST TRUMPET AND THE TUBA IN BAR 5.

EXAMPLE 2

BAR 14 THROUGH 17: THE QUINTET IS DIVIDED INTO TWO CHOIRS. THE FRENCH HORN, TROMBONE, AND TUBA UNITE IN ONE MUSICAL THOUGHT, WHILE THE TWO TRUMPETS ACCOMPANY WITH PARALLEL FANFARES.

5. Hallelujah, Amen
(from "*Judas Maccabaeus*")

Handel
(1685-1759)

6. Where'er You Walk

Handel
(1685-1759)

Bach

Cantata No. 78, for the fourteenth Sunday after Trinity, was written by Bach in Leipzig about 1740. The text of this Cantata can be summed up in the sacrifice of Christ for our redemption.

> "Thy sacrifice has cleansed the stain,
> Making my heart all pure again,
> Happy and free, happy and free."

Rarely has Bach discarded the sacred heaviness of the German Baroque music in favour of such lightness, and almost secular gaiety. The Duet is in A-B-A form, with the two trumpets taking the Soprano-Alto parts in section A, and the french horn and trombone performing that role in section B. We shall return to the details.

The Fantasia and Fugue, originally in E minor, is sub-titled 'Cathedral'. The opening nine bars seems to explore the gothic arch, while the remaining twenty-three bars of the Fantasia challenges the acoustics of the great enclosed space. As free as the Fantasia is, the Fugue is strict and structured, and exemplifies Bach at his best. Listen to our recording of the great Toccata and Fugue in D minor, and you will understand why we chose this similar but simpler selection for you.

C.B.

There are two contrasting roles and styles in the Duet. In section A to bar 50), you are the soloists. You must duplicate inflections, tone, phrases, and dynamics. You are one instrument — in two parts. But above all, you must carry a pulse set by the continuo (french horn, trombone, and tuba). Practise together and come to an agreement on interpretation. Know what the other has to play; interchange parts occasionally. Support each other, so that the running part always dominates. In bars 17, 28, and 36, pass your parts on to the other as you would in a game of catch or dodgeball. And be sensitive to Bach's "farewell", beat 2 & 3 in bar 42.

Section B starts at bar 51; you must continue to act as one instrument, but here you are part of the continuo with the tuba. Rehearse with the tuba and without the other two. (They need the time to accomplish what you have done in section A above.) Again, keep a constant pulse — never-changing, always moving forward. Straight mutes will help to keep a subservient role while modifying the tone colour. Then, return to section A, as soloists, with a new joyfulness.

7. We Hasten with Eager Footsteps

from Cantata No. 78 — Jesu, der du Meine Seele

Bach
(1685-1750)

We Hasten with Eager Footsteps *continued*

8. Fantasia and Fugue — D minor

from *Organ Works*, the 'Cathedral'

Bach
(1685-1750)

22

FUGUE

'Gloria' from the Lord Nelson Mass

JOSEPH HAYDN

Haydn was the first great master of the instrumental and orchestral style which reached its highest development in the works of Beethoven. He knew Mozart well, and taught Beethoven and many of his contemporaries. He was highly regarded in England and throughout Europe, though best of all in his native Austria.

Haydn was deeply disturbed by the French wars against his beloved Austria, and wrote two Masses (Mass in Time of War; Mass in Time of Fear). During the composition of the latter, Nelson and his British fleet defeated the French navy. When Lord Nelson and his wife toured Austria in 1800, this Mass was performed in his honour, and was re-named after him, two years after its actual completion and first performance. The 'Nelson' Mass became one of the most popular of Haydn's choral works, second only to his great oratorio, The Creation.

The 'Gloria' was originally written for soprano soloist, choir, strings, organ, three trumpets, and kettledrums. The transcription for Brass Quintet brings a new vitality to the work, without losing any of Haydn's genius.

C.B.

Alternating twin bars of accompaniment and chorus characterize the opening statement of the theme. Keep the accompaniment very light, with each and every note speaking clearly. Your turn for the solo comes at bar 25, where you must use a broader, richer tone. There is a bridge from the theme to the fugue (bar 41–47). A light singing quality is required here. As in any fugue, your presentation of the subject must copy the initial statement, first played by the trombone at bar 47. The countersubject, (what you are playing when you do not have the subject) must contrast in volume and style. The piece concludes with a return to the opening theme. Support the first trumpet while providing a rich tone for the ensemble.

9. 'Gloria' from Nelson Mass

Haydn
(1732-1809)

'Gloria' from Nelson Mass *continued*

Grand March from Aida

GUISEPPE VERDI

In 1869, Verdi, the most famous of all Italian opera composers, received an offer to write an opera on an Egyptian subject for the new theatre in Cairo to celebrate the opening of the Suez Canal. The opera was produced in Cairo on Christmas Eve, 1871. It established a new style, where the orchestra became a vital element in the drama, not just an accompaniment vehicle. The Grand March heightened the intensity of the action, and added a new force to the opera, hitherto unknown. Both from an historical perspective, and because of the rich melodies, this march has been popularized around the world. Our brass quintet transcription brings it to an even greater power and majesty.

C.B.

This will quickly become one of your favourites since the main theme, so well-known around the world, is assigned to you. But first, there are two themes as a prelude. The opening Grandioso requires full ensemble playing with excellent balance (supporting the first trumpet); the french horn's melody at bar 10 leaves you with three accented eighth notes (bars 12, 14, & 16) in partnership with the first trumpet. These must be absolutely precise; follow the first trumpet using eye contact and a strict metre. Now, beginning at the pick-up to bar 19, you present one of the world's great tunes. The breath phrases are long which is why I have marked them 'BB-Big Breath. You have detached, accented, staccato and dynamic marks. Your low D on the triplet must be tuned down; the awkward lipping must be practised over and over. Above all, play soloistically with a rich flowing tone. In rehearsal, take time at bar 69 to tune your low D with the first trumpet's high D. Watch your leader for the final cut-off.

10. Grand March from Aida

Verdi
(1813-1901)

Grand March from Aida *continued*

Jerusalem

SIR CHARLES HUBERT PARRY

Parry was the epitome of the Victorian school in England. He wrote oratorios, many anthems, church motets, four symphonies, an opera, string suites and much chamber music. But, probably the only piece that is performed often is the simple setting of William Blake's poem, 'Jerusalem', extolling the theme of the British Israelites. That is not to say that Parry is not remembered, for his pedagogical writings are still the foundation of much of our knowledge of British music.

We are pleased to include this great melody from the English Nationalistic Romantic period. It is sung as a school hymn, a World Cup Soccer rallying song, and lately was included in the film music of 'Chariots of Fire'. The solo is played in this transcription by the trombone, sometimes doubled by the french horn and the first trumpet. All the accompanying parts have a sense of flow, almost of wandering, but all must support the solo, and never overshadow that great melody. It is a difficult task, as everyone has a counter-melody within the accompaniment. This transcription, done especially for us, brings the singing qualities of the brass, together with the capabilities of rich tone and impressive dynamics, into the world of popular choral music.

Canadian Brass

11. Jerusalem

Parry
(1848-1918)

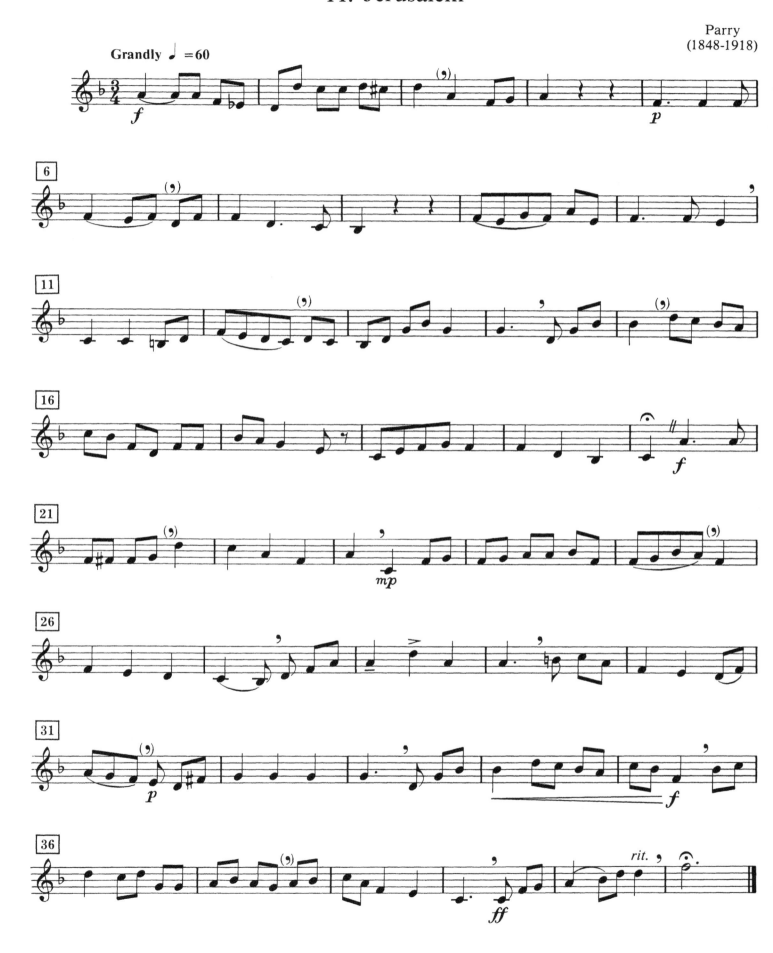

Gaudeamus Igitur

COLLEGIUM MUSICUM

This famous and very old College song originated in Europe. Its claim to immortality lies in its use by Brahms as the final theme of his 'Academic Festival Overture'. It was also incorporated into the music of 'The Student Prince', an American musical.

Verse one is treated chorally; the first trumpet plays the melody, while the other four parts support harmonically. Verse two features the french horn and the trombone doubling on the melody, while the tuba plays a step-by-step eighth note bass. Above, the two trumpets perform fanfares in dotted eighth-sixteenth rhythms. In this verse, the melody from the middle instruments must be broad and flowing in order to accentuate the staccato bass and the dotted fanfares.

This selection makes a good opening or closing piece for your concerts.

Canadian Brass

12. Gaudeamus Igitur

Collegium Musicum

Three Spirituals

Melodies from the black society of the United States are an integral part of American folk music. During the period when slavery was rampant in the southern states, Bible stories were taught through song to the illiterate. Each text told a story of emancipation from the oppressors, and the promise of eternal life and freedom with God.

The first spiritual is the well-known 'Go Down, Moses; Let My People Go'. Through the strong minor statement of the melody, one can hear the cries for liberty of the Israelites fleeing from the Egyptians. The second song is in direct contrast. 'My Lord, What A Morning' is a sublimely beautiful melody, with the words reflecting on eternal life and everlasting freedom. The arrangement ends with the stirring 'Joshua Fought The Battle Of Jericho (and the walls came tumbling down). Humourous effects depicting the falling walls are throughout the piece and add to the audience's enjoyment of the Three Spirituals.

We wish to deal with all instruments together, since these three arrangements use special effects which should be treated as a unit. For example, all five players must attack the first four bars almost with ferocity; then, they must quickly temper the dynamics and intensity in the next four bars. The trombone takes the solo line of the two verses with the upper three voices almost pleading in bars 11 and 14 for the release of the Israelites. The same mood is established in bars 21 to 24. The opening phrase of the third chorus is marked by punctuating accents in bars 33 & 34. Again, we return to an imploring mood in bars 37 to 42. Note that the french horn's note of bar 42 is held through to 43 and becomes the first note of the solo. The mood must change to one of inward peace and gentleness, sustained by the trombone and tuba entry at bar 51. The chorus, first stated by the french horn, is repeated by the entire ensemble. The melody is performed by the trombone and first trumpet, with a subtle change of line. The second spiritual concludes in a peaceful and intensely quiet ending, stated by the lower three instruments.

'Joshua' features the tuba and trombone, while the upper three instruments combine in fanfares. Watch the tuning of the open fifths, as well as the doubling at the opening, and bars 80–82. The consecutive sixths in bars 83 & 84 are very difficult to tune also, as well as the descending parts in bars 91 & 92. The french horn solo, beginning at bar 93, requires a very big and dynamic sound against the punctuating rhythm of the trumpets and trombone. The tuba must be firm and careful to keep the pulse for the others. The step sequence of the trumpets and tuba against the melody of the trombone and the 'Ram's Horn' (french horn) beginning at bar 101 is always a problem for balance and tuning, especially for the natural faults of the two trumpets in the two registers. (We have already discussed the flat high E, the sharp high G, and the need for third valve tuning of the low E flat and D.) A major problem for timing, tuning and dynamics is found in the unison section from bar 109 to bar 113. Practise slowly, combining two or three instruments, so that each player can adjust tuning throughout the phrase. Work on the first half of the concert F minor scale. Keep your dots tight and together. The ending can be made even more dramatic by the use of the glissando buzz on the upper three instruments, descending as were the walls of Jericho. Make that final chord ring in tune. We think that you will really enjoy the Three Spirituals. Incidentally, this arrangement is suited to a larger Brass Ensemble with doubling of parts as well as a Quintet.

Canadian Brass

13. Three Spirituals

Arr. Barnes

Three Spirituals *continued*

Overture to H.M.S. Pinafore

SULLIVAN

Sir Arthur Sullivan was born in England in 1842. Though he wrote some church music and popular songs ('The Lost Chord' was a favourite) his chief claim to fame was his collaboration with Sir W.S.Gilbert in the composition of twelve operettas. Almost all of these works satirized the patronage and class system of 19th century England. The D'Oyly Carte Opera Company was set up for the express purpose of protecting and performing the G. & S. works, and held those rights until recently. All the operettas have the same humourous plots, and the same very specific manner of performance. It is suggested that students listen to an authentic recording by D'Oyly Carte, or see one of the operettas on the stage or television. This will help very much in the interpretation of the Overture.

Any performance of the music of Sullivan must follow a certain style: lightness, gaiety, detached accompaniment. The melodies are almost frivolous, and must be performed in a jocular manner. Even the sentimental song by the french horn at bar 52 must have a quality of exaggeration.

The drum-roll opening (tuba and trombone doubled) leads in a mighty crescendo to the opening song (first trumpet on the melody, but traded about as it would be on stage from singer to singer). Every player *must* perform in a very detached manner, bringing every four bars to a semicolon, and every eight bars to a period. Find as much contrast and drama as possible in every part.

Bar 45 begins the bridge to the french horn aria at bar 52. The accompaniment should be very delicate and well below the volume of the french horn. The first trumpet doubles the french horn at bar 65, just as a soprano joins a tenor on stage. Watch the timing in bar 70; the first trumpet and french horn move together *after* the second trumpet and trombone move together. The third melody begins at bar 72. First, there is a dialogue between the two trumpets; later, at bar 103, the dialogue is among four instruments. The melody at bar 111 is the beginning of a dance, so keep it spritely, lively, and detached (again, at 128). The finale starts at bar 136 and carries on, almost with reckless abandon, to the final punctuating chords at bars 175–179.

We think that this is the first time that a brass quintet has had the opportunity to perform G. & S. We hope that you and your audiences enjoy the experience.

Canadian Brass

14. Overture to 'H.M.S. Pinafore'

Sullivan
(1842-1900)

Overture to 'H.M.S. Pinafore' *continued*

Overture to 'H.M.S. Pinafore' *continued*

A Note on Performance

We hope that many of you have progressed through both the *Beginning* and the *Easy* books in our Educational Series, and have taken note of the final pages on performance. The points that we drew to your attention, though simply expressed, are as true now as then.

"Don't choose to play a piece that you cannot guarantee — under stress of a public concert — success. Choose pieces from the book that your group can perform well . . ."

"Choose a variety of pieces, thinking of tempos, dynamics, keys, and who has the melody."

from the Canadian Brass Book of Beginning Quintets

"The listeners are not present to hear technical achievement; they want a pleasant selection of music. The good performer never allows the audience to notice technical difficulties, so choose music well within the group's capabilities . . ."

"The performance begins as you enter, and finishes when you leave. Be aware of all visual details and keep distraction to a minimum."

from the Canadian Brass Book of Easy Quintets

We hope that, when planning your public performances, you will keep these notes in mind.

As well, good encore selections, which should always be simple considering that your initial energy will have been somewhat depleted, can be found in the BEGINNING Book (Battle Hymn of the Republic, or St. Anthony Chorale) and in the EASY Book (El Yivneh Hagalil — featuring the Tuba, or, The Lord Bless You and Keep You). Your self-confidence, your awareness to detail, and your communication within your group will enable you to perform to the "Optimum" for the great satisfaction of your audience, and the greater satisfaction of your quintet and yourself.

'Enjoy'

The Canadian Brass

Next Step: The Canadian Brass Brassworks Series — selections from the world's finest brass quintet music.